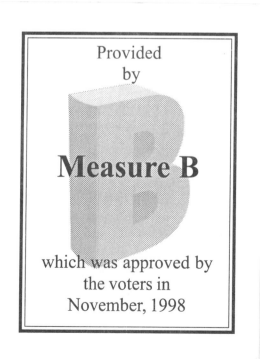

Provided
by

Measure B

which was approved by
the voters in
November, 1998

Fractions

This math series is dedicated to Nick, Tony, Riley, and Hailey.

Published by The Child's World®
PO Box 326
Chanhassen, MN 55317-0326
800-599-READ
www.childsworld.com

Design and Production:
The Creative Spark, San Juan Capistrano, CA
Photos: © David M. Budd Photography.

Library of Congress Cataloging-in-Publication Data
Pistoia, Sara.
   Fractions / by Sara Pistoia.
        p. cm. — (Mighty math series)
Includes index.
Summary: Simple text explains fractions, what they are, and how
to use them.
   ISBN 1-56766-113-0 (lib. bdg. : alk. paper)
   1. Fractions—Juvenile literature. [1. Fractions.] I. Title. II.
Series.
   QA117 .P57 2002
   513.2'6—dc21

                                        2002004945

MIGHTY MATH

Fractions

Sara Pistoia

The Child's World

People everywhere use fractions. Fractions show how many parts of something make up the whole. Fractions can help us be fair when we share.

Hi! I'm Math Mutt! I'm here to help you learn about fractions. Do you know that two halves equal a whole?

This candy bar is a whole.

Let's cut it in two, right down the middle. Now there are two equal parts. Each part is a fraction called one-half.

one-half + one-half = a whole

Four friends have pie for dessert.
How can they share it?

This way isn't very fair.

This way is better. Each friend
gets one-fourth of the pie.

This pie has four equal pieces.
That's the fair way to share!

Here is some other foods cut into parts.

This pizza is cut into three equal parts. Each part is called one-third.

Remember, a fraction must have equal parts. When you share, be fair! Make fractions.

This apple is cut into
two equal parts.
Each part is one-half.

This pear is cut into
two parts that are
not equal. Neither
part is one-half.

Is this sandwich
cut into fractions?

Fractions can be equal parts of a group, too. You could share this group of six cookies with two friends. Don't forget yourself!

If you divide the cookies into three equal parts, each friend can have two cookies. Each person's share is one-third of the whole pile.

When bakers make cookies, they use fractions.

They use one whole egg.

They use one whole cup of flour.

But the rest of the
ingredients are
fractions: one-half
cup of sugar,

one-fourth cup
of butter,

and one-half
teaspoon of salt.

Here are some other fractions.
One-fourth of these flowers
are pink. What fraction of the
flowers are yellow?

There are four flowers. Each
flower equals one-fourth.

one-fourth

three-fourths

15

You can use words and pictures to talk about fractions. You can use numerals, too.

I think 3/4 of these blocks are red.

one-fourth = $^1/_4$

three-fourths = $^3/_4$

We often use numerals to show fractions.

$$\frac{1}{2}$$

The bottom numeral shows how many parts are in the whole thing. The top numeral shows how many of those parts we are talking about.

$\frac{1}{3}$

This stoplight has three parts. One light is on. The other two lights are off.

$\frac{2}{3}$

One-third of the stoplight is on.
Two-thirds of the stoplight is off.

Here are ten bowling pins.

A ball knocks down five pins.
Five pins are still standing.
What fraction of the pins
fell down?

There are two equal parts. Five pins are standing, and five pins have fallen. Five pins are one-half of the whole. One-half ($1/2$) of the pins fell down.

So remember your fractions.
Be fair when you share.

May I have one of those cookies?

Your friends will know just how much you care!

Key Words

divide

equal

fraction

one-fourth ($\frac{1}{4}$)

one-half ($\frac{1}{2}$)

one-third ($\frac{1}{3}$)

part

three-fourths ($\frac{3}{4}$)

two-thirds ($\frac{2}{3}$)

whole

Index

About the Author

Sara Pistoia is a retired elementary teacher living in Southern California with her husband and a variety of pets. After 40 years of teaching, she now contributes to education by supervising and training student teachers at California State University at Fullerton. In authoring this series, she draws on the experience of many years of teaching first and second graders.

1068058880